# I AM THERE

—RADHIKA KAILASH MORYANI

This is the work of poetry, Names, Characters, businesses, places, events, and incidents are either products of the poet's imagination or used in a non-fiction manner. Any resemble to actual persons, living or dead, or actual events is purely co-incidental.

First Edition: August 2025

Printed in India

ISBN: **978-93-343-8587-8**

# Dedication

To the quiet eyes that watched me, fall and rise— the breath of the mountains, the prayer of my Dadi, and the grace that never left, even when I did. To every girl who walks the barefoot., yet carries galaxies within— may you remember:

**You are not alone;**
**You are not forgotten.**
**You are always there.**

With love,

Radhika Kailash Moryani.

# Prologue

There were days I couldn't hear my own name.

The world grew loud. I grew smaller.

And yet, in the hush between my breaths,

something whispered—not to give up.

This book is not about healing.

It is about remembering.

Not who I wanted to be,

but who I had always been:

soft, intuitive, watchful—

with hands that knew silence, and eyes that trusted God.

Every chapter you read is a mirror.

Sometimes it will show you your pain. Other times, your freedom.

But always, always—it will remind you:

There is a presence within you that never leaves.

You may call it love.

Or life.

Or simply, I Am There.

# Contents

# Part One: In The Mire

## [ Inner Turmoil]

I began my book with Inner Turmoil because that is where every soul's true journey begins. Before we learn to embrace light, we must first face the shadows within us.

The mire represents life's hardships—the doubts, heartbreaks, and scattered dreams that weigh us down. It is in these moments of confusion that we often lose sight of who we are. But just as the lotus blooms only in muddy waters, our resilience and inner beauty emerge from these struggles.

Inner Turmoil is not written to dwell in sorrow, but to honour honesty. It reminds us that healing does not begin in perfection, but in brokenness. By facing our inner battles, we open the path toward freedom, love, and clarity.

This is why Part One exists: to show that even in the deepest turmoil lies the seed of transformation.

# "I am not their version of me"

They thought I'd explain myself.
That I'd defend my softness.
That I'd fight to fix
the version of me they carry in their mind.
But I've grown silent – not in fear, in peace.
I see the game, but I don't play.
I hear the taunts, but I don't echo.
I know their patterns, and I choose not to dance.
Their silence doesn't scare me.
Their gatherings don't unsettle me.
Their twisted smiles are not my reflection.
I am not their version of me.
I am the story they couldn't rewrite.
Not their silence, Not their smallness,
Not their shame.
I am still. I am sure.
I am free – and that is enough.

## “What they didn’t know, I was healing’’

They thought I was distant.
They thought I was cold.
They whispered that I changed.
And maybe I did.
But what they didn’t see
was the quiet war I was fighting—
the slow stitching of wounds,
they never cared to understand.
I wasn’t avoiding them.
I was returning to myself.
I wasn’t silent for drama.
I was learning how to breathe again
without breaking.
In rooms where I once felt unseen,
I no longer searched for light.
I became it.

They measured me by my absence,
judged me by their stories—
but healing is never loud.
It happens when no one is watching.
I let go of proving.
I let go of pleasing.
I let go of the girl
who thought she had to earn love.
And somewhere, in that gentle shedding,
I met the woman I was always meant to be.

## “The boundaries that saved me”

I always knew.
Even when their words smiled, my soul flinched.
They thought they hid it well—the lies, the gossip,
The little ways they tried to shrink my spirit.
But I was never blind.
I just stayed soft longer than I should have.
It wasn’t kindness that kept me quiet.
It was shock.
That someone could pretend so well,
and harm so easily.
They thought my silence was weakness.
It wasn’t.
It was the moment I built my first boundary
without noise—only truth.
I didn’t stretch into them.
I stood still.
And the stillness revealed everything.
They mocked, provoked, called my calm dramatic.
But I saw through them—and that ruined their game.

My peace became their discomfort.
My clarity, their fear.
Boundaries didn't make me bitter.
They made me free.
And from that day forward, I stopped giving access
to those who only came to rewrite my worth.

# "The Power of Quiet"

They expected noise, when I chose myself.
They waited for anger,
for rebellion, for the storm they thought they'd caused.
But I gave them nothing.
No shouts. No speeches.
Just stillness and the sound of my soul returning home.
Quiet is not weakness.
It is the breath held between pain and peace.
It is the choice to step back without stepping down.
I have nothing to prove.
No image to fix. No drama to feed.
I am not reacting— because I am healing.
I am not loud— because I am listening to my own becoming.
This silence they mock?
It is sacred. It is strong. It is mine.

## “HER Absence Was Her Answer”

She didn’t shout. She didn’t explain.
She simply stopped showing up
where her soul felt unseen.
They thought she was bitter—
but she was just done. Done waiting, done trying,
done justifying her presence
to people who misused it.
She didn’t leave with a storm.
She left like the tide—soft, quiet, certain.
Her absence said all the things her mouth had grown
tired of repeating.
She didn’t need to slam the door.
She just walked away
and let the silence seal it shut.
They still talk, still gather, still perform.
But they feel it now—
the space she once held,
and the peace she took with her.

Because she didn't leave in anger.
She left in clarity.
And that made her absence
impossible to ignore.

## “And Still, She Rose”

They tried to define her by the mess they made.
By the silence they caused.
By the weight they left.
But she wasn’t made to stay broken.
She was made to bloom, even in the dark.
There were nights she folded into herself—
grief pressing against her chest,
memories louder than peace.
But even then, a small light inside her whispered,
Not here. Not forever.
She wasn’t loud in her return.
She didn’t come back for applause.
She came back for herself—
for the girl who once begged to be understood,
and the woman who no longer needs to be.
They didn’t offer apologies.
They didn’t give closure.
But she gave herself freedom.

And that was enough.
She learned that rising isn't always standing tall.
Sometimes it's standing quietly without shrinking.
And so, she rose— with softer eyes, stronger bones,
and a heart that now beats for her.

## "This Softness Took Strength"

They saw the calm in her eyes
and thought life had been kind.
They mistook her grace
for a life without bruises.
But softness is not what she was given—
it's what she chose, again and again,
even when the world offered her every reason to
harden.
She doesn't raise her voice anymore.
Not because she can't—
but because peace is her home now.
She protects it like sacred ground.
Her gentleness is not weakness.
It is power wrapped in quiet.
It is steel beneath silk.
She has cried alone
and smiled in rooms where she wasn't safe.

She has walked away from the need to be understood,
and found her belonging within.
She doesn't need to prove her strength.
It's in the way she listens.
It's in the way she forgives without losing herself.
Her softness is her boundary.
Her silence is her knowing.
Her stillness is her strength.
And when they ask, "How are you still so kind?"
She smiles— Because I healed the storm,
and chose to be the sky.

# Part Two: The Becoming

## [Awakening & Acceptance]

# 🌿 Part Two – The Art of Letting Be

In this part, the struggle begins to soften.
After facing the storm within, there comes a quiet shift — the realization that not everything needs to be controlled or carried.

Here, the journey is about acceptance and release. It's not about forgetting the pain, but about learning to let it breathe, to give space for healing.

These reflections speak of forgiveness, surrender, and trust — allowing life to unfold as it must. In letting things "be," we start finding the peace that was waiting all along.

# "My body, My temple"

My body is not a battlefield.
It is a temple.
I no longer punish it to please others.
I no longer shrink to fit their silence.
I listen to it now – with love.
I feed it when it's hungry.
I rest when it's tired.
I dress for myself.
I move with joy.
This body held me through pain,
carried me when I had no words,
and still stood tall.
I no longer judge it. I honour it.
I bow to it –because it is mine.

# "He Was with Me All Along"

When I couldn't rise, You held my breath.
When I couldn't speak, You heard my silence.
There were days when I wondered if You had left
me—
when life broke me in quiet corners and no one saw.
But even then, You were working.
Not loudly. Not quickly.
But always with love.
You didn't remove the storm.
You became my shelter.
You didn't answer every prayer—
You became my strength to wait.
I didn't walk this path alone.
You held my feet steady
when I had no strength to trust the ground.
Through every betrayal, You gave me wisdom.
Through every loss,
You returned me to myself.

And now, as I stand—
softer, stronger, freer—
I know the truth:
You were with me.
You are with me.
You will always be with me.
I am not alone.
I never was.

# “A Letter to My Younger Self”

From Radhika,
(Who bloomed in the mire)

Dear Younger Me,
You never knew it would be this hard. That love would come wrapped in silence, and pain would wear a familiar face. You didn’t know the ones you trusted would try to control your light, break your spirit, or provoke you just to watch you fall apart. And still, you tried. You gave chances.
You spoke kindly, even when it hurt. You said sorry just to save the peace. But you didn’t fail, my dear. You were walking through a pattern you didn’t even know existed.
You were facing narcissism with a heart that only knew how to love. You wanted to call out the wrong. You wanted to explain the truth. Because that’s what human nature teaches us—to speak up, to say, “This is not right. “But every time you did, they turned it back on you. They wanted your anger—so, they could twist

it into blame. And so, with the grace of the Divine, you did the hardest thing—you stopped reacting. You chose silence over shouting.

You chose God over ego. You chose to rise without noise. And in that sacred stillness, you broke the pattern. Yes, it hurt. Yes, it was lonely. But you learned to walk through fire without letting it burn your truth. Your faith saved you. Your God walked beside you. And even in the dark, your soul kept whispering, "Keep going. "Maybe this was a soul contract—one you were meant to complete or finally break. Only the Divine knows. But today, I thank even the pain. Because it carved the woman I am now. You made it. With your faith. With your softness. With your unshaken trust in the Universe. And if I could hold your hand then,

I would say—You don't need to fight to prove yourself. You don't need to shout to be heard. Your peace will speak for you. And your God will never leave you. With love, pride, and deep gratitude,

**Your Future Self,**

**Radhika Kailash**

**The girl who bloomed through grace, not approval — and rose because her roots reached the Divine.**

# I set you free

*"I promise you will recognise yourself in every life as you capture yourself as your fragrance of love."*

There was a time when we loved deeply, but life has a way of transforming love—sometimes shifting it away from others and even from ourselves. Along the way, we often lose sight of whose truly are. People say that life's purpose is found in living for others, but that doesn't mean abandoning our own happiness. We can care for others without sacrificing the love we owe ourselves.

But what does happiness truly mean? It looks different for everyone. Moments of joy are fleeting, and time never stands still. While we can shape our future, we can't undo the past. We dream and make promises—to others and to ourselves—but as life changes, those dreams sometimes
shatter, leaving us broken. We feel lost, as if the pieces of our lives have scattered beyond our grasp.

When someone leaves, we must let them go. We hold onto the memories—the good and the painful—but in truth, we can't know where those people are now or what they've become. Time reshapes those memories, turning heartbreak into lessons and joy into nostalgia. We should

honour those memories, but not let them chain us to the past. They're a part of us, but they don't determine our future.

Yes, we may feel scattered, our dreams left behind. But we must gather those broken pieces and rebuild. We must reclaim the promises we made to ourselves. And when the time comes, if someone from our past looks back, they will see the person we've become—someone who found

their freedom, even if it meant leaving behind what was once familiar.

They might say, "You knew this journey would take you far from me, but you also knew one day you'd look back at all we shared."

But whether someone from your past returns or not, your happiness will find you again. When you rediscover self-love and pursue the dreams you once thought unreachable, you'll be truly free.

This journey will teach you resilience, forgiveness, and clarity. You'll learn the power of letting go, of freeing yourself from doubt and embracing courage. You'll discover that life's greatest lesson is staying true to yourself. And with that knowledge, you'll face whatever comes next and achieve what you once thought was out of reach.

As you walk this path, you'll realize that you've always been enough. Your happiness, your dreams, are like a beautiful melody played just for you. You'll become the radiant person you were meant to be—the guardian of your own life, turning your desires into reality. You'll bloom like a rare flower in the secret garden of your heart.

So, set yourself free. Step out of the quiet room where you've been hiding and into the world. I promise, when you do, you'll find yourself in every breath, every dream, every moment. You'll see that the essence of love was within you all along, and in that recognition, you'll find a freedom that's truly yours.

Set yourself free, and you'll discover the love you've been searching for—the love that has always been within you.

# I CLOSE MY EYES

*"The World Within Awaits"*

I close my eyes, and galaxies bloom within,
A quiet cosmos where dreams begin.
Stars weave stories in threads of light,
Guiding my soul through the endless night.
The moon whispers secrets of tides untamed,
Planets hum songs that cannot be named.
Within this vast and boundless expanse,
I find my strength in the cosmic dance.
The sun of my heart burns steady and bright,
A beacon of hope, my eternal light.
Comets of thought blaze through the sky,
As questions dissolve, I no longer ask "why."
Each star is a lesson, each nebula a scar,
Proof that I've journeyed, near and far.
The universe within reflects the one outside,
A mirror of truth where fears cannot hide.

In the depths of the void, I see my place,
A speck of dust, yet infinite in grace.
I close my eyes, and galaxies bloom within—
Here, I am whole. Here, I begin.

# RISE & SHINE

*"A Story of Resilience and Growth"*

Through whispered doubts and voices loud,
I stand alone, unbroken, proud.
The paths I've walked, the words I've known,
Have only made my spirit grow.
They tried to dim my inner light,
But in their shadows, I took flight.
No longer bound by what they say,
I choose my path, come what may.
The world can speak, the world can judge,
But I won't let their words be a grudge.
For in my heart, I hold the key,
To live with love and positivity.
In every step, I feel them near,
My parents' love, my husband's cheer.
With their support, I rise above,
Their faith in me, my strength, my love.
My parents' hands, they showed me the way,
Taught me love, and taught me to stay.

In their wisdom, I find my grace,
A foundation built; time cannot erase.
They taught me well, through pain and strife,
To not take blame for others' lies.
For wounds they caused, I would not bear,
Their burden's not mine, I choose to care.
So onward I go, with steady grace,
Running towards my brighter space.
For life is mine, and I will be,
The one I'm meant to always see.

# A BUTTERFLY AT MY DOOR

*"A Moment with the Butterfly"*

I found a butterfly at my door,
It hovered gently, seeking more—
A quiet wish to venture in,
Yet lingered still, unsure to begin.
Its fragile wings held stories untold,
A masterpiece of colours bold.
It danced upon the breath of air,
A fleeting guest, beyond compare.
I stepped inside, the door closed slow,
Hoping it wouldn't harm nor go.
But then, a thought—a gentle tide,
I turned back, leaving the door open wide.
There it lay, on the floor so near,
As if awaiting me to appear.
Its silent plea, its graceful stay,
Bore a mystery word couldn't convey.
The air from the door, it softly stirred,
Yet the butterfly moved not, nor blurred.

Its fragile grip upon the floor,
A delicate soul, yearning for more.
I cupped it softly in my hand,
A bridge between two fragile lands.
I asked, "Who are you? What's your tale?"
But silence met my quiet hail.
Its beauty spoke, in colours bright,
Wings of stained glass kissed by light.
In that moment, time stood still,
A wonder sparked, beyond my will.
The lens of my eye, I turned to view,
Captured its hues in waves of blue.
Reflections danced, a story grew,
A creature of grace, born anew.
A symbol, a sign, what could it be?
A messenger sent, just for me?
A fleeting bond, yet deep and true—
The butterfly whispered, and away it flew.

# Unfolding in Stillness

*"Where Silence Heals and Strength Blooms"*

Beneath the storm of clashing sound,
A gentle stillness can be found.
Where echoes fade and shadows blend,
The quiet heart begins to mend.
The chaos stirs, the world may fray,
But silence carves another way.
A refuge deep, untouched by strife,
A softer rhythm, the pulse of life.
Some voices rise, their edges sharp,
To cut the strings of kindness' harp.
Their words, like arrows, seek to sting,
Yet silence hums—a timeless ring.
In the stillness, the soul takes flight,
Weaving verses through the night.
Where anger falters, fades, and dies,
Peace whispers back in soft replies.
Like a flower in the murky tide,
Unmoved by currents, it will bide.

Its roots sink deep, its petals glow,
Unaffected by what others throw.
The mud may cling, the storms may roar,
But the bloom persists, forever more.
Its beauty thrives in the murky ground,
A quiet triumph, profound and sound.
Let them speak, let tempests flare,
A deeper strength is cultivated there.
For every thorn, a lesson grows, each scar, a map of what one knows.
The river bends, the winds will turn,
In silent depths, new truths we learn.
The whispers guide, the echoes call,
Through stillness, one transcends it all.
For those who pause, who let things be,
Discover the path to harmony.
Not in the clash, nor in the fight,
But in the quiet, they find their light.
So let the storm rage loud and strong,
Its noise won't linger, not for long.
In stillness deep, the heart remains,
Unfolding softly, breaking chains.
Through silence blooms a lasting grace,

A steadfast soul, time can't erase.

A whisper heard when the noise is done—

A quiet strength, a battle won.

# ECHOES OF HER FLAME

*"Strength Found in the Shadows"*

In a world of murmurs and shadowed hues,
A tender spark began to lose.
The air was thick with twisted tones,
Seeking to carve her into stones.
The winds would pull, the ground would quake,
Her fragile steps would often break.
Yet deep within, a flicker stayed,
Unyielding to the games they played.
The skies grew heavy, the nights stretched long,
But silence taught her to be strong.
No need for words, no need to fight,
Her path lay hidden in the night. Through restless storms and bitter rain,
She learned to temper every pain.
Her roots sank deep, her branches reached,
Far beyond where shadows preached.
Time became her quiet guide,
A patient river by her side.
She found her strength in still retreat,

And built a world they couldn’t beat.
Now she rises, unseen by most,
A quiet triumph, a whispered boast.
Her light burns steady, calm, and true,
A flame that shadows never knew.

# A FLOW OF GRACE

*"We learn through fire, and we grow."*

In a crowded room, a child so small,
Reaches for the glass, unaware of it all.
The tea within, too hot to hold,
Yet tiny fingers, brave and bold.
No knowledge of heat, no sense of fear,
Just curious eyes, watching near.
He sees the hands of those he loves,
And tries to mimic from above.
In that moment, innocence shines,
Unaware of life's unseen lines.
The burn may come, the lesson learned,
But growth arrives where fingers yearn.
And so, it is for the girl so new,
In a house or job, with skies unknown blue. She steps
with care, her heart unsure,
Through doors of life that feel so pure.
No guide to warn of what's too hot,
She tries, she fails, she gives a lot.

Just like the child, she reaches out,
Unaware of the coming doubt.
For when we touch what we don't yet know,
We learn through fire, and we grow.
In burns and stumbles, wisdom wakes,
In love and life, the heart remakes.
Both child and woman, side by side,
In a world where innocence and pride collide.
They'll hold the heat, they'll feel the cold,
But through it all, they'll both grow bold.

# THE ETERNAL FRAGRANCE

"Hold close the joy, the love, the glow,
And let the fragrant memories grow."

A flower blooms in morning light,
With colours bold, so pure, so bright.
Its petals soft, its scent so sweet,
A gentle song, a rhythmic beat.
But even beauty, full of grace,
Must one day vanish, leave no trace.
No matter how it shines today,
Its petals soon will fall away.
Yet when its bloom has come and gone,
Its fragrance lingers on and on.
A tender breeze, a whispered tune,
That fills the air beneath the moon.
For once, it graced your world with light,
And turned your darkness into bright.
Its scent, a memory soft and kind,
Will live forever in your mind.
Though time may steal its lovely hue,
Its gentle essence stays with you.

A perfume of the love it gave,
Still dancing on, beyond the grave.
So, when the petals start to fall,
Don't mourn the loss of beauty's call.
The flower's song will always play,
In every breeze, in every day.
Hold close the joy, the love, the glow,
And let the fragrant memories grow.
For though the bloom may fade from sight,
Its song will fill your heart with light.

# Part: Three

# I AM THERE
# [Oneness & Surrender]

## ✨ Part Three – Oneness & Surrender

This is the flowering after the mire. Having walked through turmoil and release, you step into the space of clarity, self-love, and divine connection.

Here, the words rise lighter — carrying hope, faith, and the beauty of discovering your true essence. It is about recognizing that the love and strength you sought outside were always within.

Part Three is a celebration of becoming whole, of walking freely with grace, and of embracing the spiritual truth: "I am there."

# THE SUN WILL RISE

*"A Journey of Light, Hope, and Resilience."*

Each morning breaks with golden light,
And chases off the fading night.
The sunrise makes me pause and see,
That no matter what, it's there for me.
Though life may bring its ebb and flow,
And people come, then quickly go,
The sun will rise, both calm and true,
To paint the sky with colours new.
In moments when I feel alone,
With shadows deep, the way unknown,
The sun appears, a guiding hand,
To brighten paths, I hadn't planned.
It doesn't ask for thanks or praise,
Yet warms my soul on colder days.
A faithful friend that lights my way,
Through every storm, it finds a way.
Even when the clouds are grey,

Hiding skies where sunbeams play,
I know behind those veils of gloom,
The sun will always find its bloom.
For whether love stands by my side,
Or fleeting footsteps fail to bide,
The sun will come, as it always does,
A gift from life, a gentle buzz.
It teaches me, without a word,
That faith and hope are never blurred.
For every dawn, with steady flame,
Reminds me that I'm still the same.
So even if the world turns cold,
And all my stories left untold,
The sun will rise, no matter when—
To fill my heart with light again.
In each bright ray, a promise stays:
That I am strong in many ways.
No matter who may come or flee, the sun will shine,
and I'll be free.

# BENEATH THE VIOLET SKY

*"Solace in moments of need."*

In a vibrant city by the sea, lived a girl named Aria,
Her heart expansive, like the sky's wide area.
Amid the city's rush, she felt a gentle pull,
To a café where kindness made her heart full.
Inside the café, where the hustle paused,
Aria found a world where warmth never lost.
The owner, modest and never seeking fame,
Used the café's earnings to help, without a name.
They funded dreams, eased burdens from afar,
Their generosity flowed like rain from the stars.
In the café's corners, a mentor's quiet grace,
Guided and nurtured in a subtle embrace.
Compassionate hands, in times of need,
Offered solace and care, a gentle creed.
Their kindness was like waves that soothe and mend,
Bringing warmth and peace to those they tended.
Community builders, working in the shade,
Organized help, ensuring no one was delayed.
Their efforts wove a fabric strong and true,

Binding hearts together with a caring view.
Silent advocates fought for justice, unbent,
Their work was a quiet, unending commitment.
Like the sky's vast reach, their influence spread,
Changing the world in ways often unsaid. One day, a stranger, with a smile so bright,
Paid for Aria's meal, a simple delight.
This fleeting act, like a star in the night,
Reminded her of kindness in soft, glowing light.
Aria learned to see the hidden grace,
In acts of kindness that time cannot erase.
Like the sky's silent watch over the sea,
True support and love are often quietly free.
Carrying these lessons, she embraced the view,
That the deepest kindness comes from the unseen, true.
Just like the sky's endless, gentle embrace,
Unseen helpers make the world a better place.

# THE LIGHT INSIDE

"A journey of self discovery."

In a village quiet and serene,
Lived Madhavi, with a heart unseen.
Her soul yearned for love's embrace,
She sought its form in every place.
Through bustling streets and distant lands,
In city lights and foreign sands,
She chased a vision, rare and bright,
Believing love was out of sight.
But with each quest, a piece would fade,
her essence lost; her spirit swayed.
In endless search, she drifted far,
Yet love remained a distant star.
One evening by a tranquil lake,
The sunset's hues began to break.
Madhavi, weary from her quest,
Found solace where the waters rest.
An elder, wise with years gone by,
Approached her with a knowing eye.

"Why do you seek love so in vain?"
The woman asked, easing her pain.
"I search for love in every face,"
Madhavi sighed, "but lose my place.
Each time I think I've touched its grace,
I lose a part, a fleeting trace."
The elder smiled, serene and kind,
"Love's not a prize for you to find.
It's not a treasure to behold,
But warmth within, a light of gold."
"Instead of seeking far and wide,
Turn inward to where love resides.
Embrace your soul, your essence true,
For love begins and ends with you."
With hands entwined in gentle care,
The elder's touch, a soothing air,
Madhavi felt a spark ignite,
A truth revealed in soft moonlight.
She began to love her heart's own beat,
In self-reflection, joy complete.
No longer lost, she found her grace,
In self-love's warm and tender embrace.
Her heart now shone with light so pure,

Love flowed from her, strong and sure.
She lived from within, her spirit bright,
Her inner love a guiding light.
Thus, Madhavi learned, as all must see,
Love starts within, in you and me.
For in embracing our own heart's hue,
The love we seek is born anew.

# THE DESIRES OF WOMAN

"She wishes to bloom like flowers."

They laughed at her dreams. Her desires were brushed aside as trivial, fanciful things, as if a woman's wishes should always fit within narrow expectations. But deep inside, she held a fire that refused to be extinguished.

From a young age, she had longed for more. Not just more possessions or success, but more life —more depth, more meaning. She wanted to feel the world with every fibre of her being, to stretch her arms wide and embrace all it had to offer. She dreamed of a life untethered, free to bloom like wildflowers in an open field, her soul whispering her truths like the wind dancing through trees.

Each day, she carried within her a myriad of desires, some small and fleeting, others vast and profound. She longed for love, for the kind of companionship that didn't stifle her, but nurtured her growth. A

partner who would listen, not just to her words, but to the spaces between them,
the silence where her deepest thoughts lived. She wanted someone who would see her not just as she appeared, but as she truly was, in all her layers and complexities. Yet, when she dared speak her dreams, they laughed. “Be realistic,” they said. “That’s too much to ask for.” But how could it be too much? How could a woman’s desire to be loved, understood, and free be too much?

Still, she pressed on. Each laugh, each scoff, only fuelled her determination. She kept her heart open, waiting for the moment when her desires would be met—not by someone else, but by herself first. For she realized that before she could expect others to see her, she had to truly see
herself.

So, she began to live for herself, chasing her dreams with a quiet but fierce determination. She wrote down her thoughts, allowing her pen to flow like a river, carving out new paths for her heart. She surrounded herself with beauty, letting nature's symphony remind her of the life she craved.

And slowly, piece by piece, she became the woman she had always desired to be. And then, one day, when she least expected it, she met someone. A gem, not because they completed her, but because they understood her. They listened—not with the intent to respond, but with the intent to hear. They encouraged her to soar, to chase the stars she had once been told were out of reach.

In them, she found a reflection of her own strength. They didn't clip her wings, but watched her fly, their love wrapping around her like a soft breeze, always present, never constraining.

Together, they created a world where her desires were no longer laughed at, but celebrated.

In the end, her story wasn't just about finding love—it was about finding the courage to pursue her desires, regardless of what others thought. It was about learning that her wishes, no matter how big or small, were valid and worthy. And most of all, it was about discovering that the greatest fulfilment came not from being understood by others, but from truly understanding herself.

# IN HIS FIST

*"She's safe in all eternity."*

She stands by the valley, quiet and still,
Where nature bends to the Master's will.
Her wide eyes gleam with wonder's light,
Framed by the valley's breath-taking sight.
The sky above begins to say,
How nature blooms in her own way,
"Look at this girl, so pure and bright,
Cradled softly in my endless flight.
The Master's hands have spread so wide,
Guarding her from every side.
With every breeze and every tree,
His fingers hold her tenderly.
The rivers run, the hills arise,
To watch her grow beneath these skies.
The earth beneath her feet is strong,
A song of love that's ages long.
Each leaf that flutters in the air,
Is a promise that He's always there.

His fingers stretch, the winds they sing,
And wrap her in His covering.
This girl, this beauty with eyes so wide,
Is held by the One who made the skies.
Protected here, by earth and sea,
She's safe in all eternity."
She stands in awe, her heart at rest,
Knowing she's loved, protected, blessed.
The valley hums, the sky looks on,
Her soul embraced by the Eternal One.

# I DONT SEARCH ME, HE TOOK FORM

*"Untangle the knots that bind me tight,*
*Let my steps be filled with light."*

There was once a woman standing at the crossroads of her life. The road ahead was shrouded in fog, leaving her unsure of where to go or how to proceed. She had always been strong, but now, as she faced the unknown, she felt a quiet whisper of doubt growing within her.

"Lord, show me the path," she prayed softly, her voice carrying a mix of longing and uncertainty.
"I don't know what is right or wrong anymore. I feel lost." She looked at the world around her and saw people rushing by, each seemingly sure of where they were headed. But deep down, she knew that many were just as unsure as she was, hiding their confusion behind hurried steps and busy lives. She didn't want to live that way—moving forward blindly, without purpose.

"Lead me to places where I can truly see," she prayed again. "Let me witness the colours of kinship, the beauty of understanding and trust. Help me find my way to those who can guide me, those who will offer wisdom and love without condition."

She closed her eyes, imagining herself as a sage—calm, wise, and discerning. But wisdom, she knew, didn't come easily. It required patience and the ability to trust in something greater than herself. "Lord, let me know whom to trust," she whispered. "Guide me toward the hearts that are genuine, the souls that will help me grow."

The fog around her seemed to swirl, untangling slightly, as if the universe was listening to her plea. But the road still stretched far beyond her sight, and the way forward remained unclear. "Untangle the knots of my life," she continued, her hands clasped tightly in prayer. "Show me where I need to go. I seek not perfection, but an ideal that allows me to live fully, with grace and understanding. I want to walk a path that leads me toward my highest self, where flaws are not failures, but lessons."

As she stood there, waiting for an answer, she realized that the journey was never about finding the perfect road or making every decision right. It was about trusting the process, having faith that with each step, the path would reveal itself. The fog that once seemed so thick now
appeared less menacing, as if it were lifting little by little.

In that moment, she felt a quiet sense of peace settle within her. The answers she sought weren't written in the sky, nor were they handed to her by some unseen force. The answers were within her, waiting for her to trust in the journey. "I may not know where I am headed," she thought, "but I will walk with courage. I will walk with
faith."

And so, with a heart open to the unknown and a prayer on her lips, she took the first step. The
path ahead still curved into the distance, but now she walked it with the quiet assurance that she

was not alone. The Lord was guiding her—not by showing her every turn, but by giving her the strength to find her way.

## *Baby, I Won't Judge You*

## *(A Song for The Soul)*

Baby, I won't judge you,

Come to me, let your heart be true.

Whenever you feel the weight of the day,

Burst your anger, let it all out and stay.

Hit your aggression, don't hold back,

I'm dense, I'll cover every crack.

Let your storm rage, let it unfold,

In my embrace, let your story be told.

Oh baby, I won't judge you,

In my arms, your worries will find a view.

I'll conserve your trust, filter your dreams,

Clean up the threats, and stitch up the seams.

I'm the habitat where angels play,

A sanctuary where fears decay.

I'll serve you a life of joy and light,

Where everything's clear and nothing's out of sight.

Oh darling, you're a treasure so rare,

Your values in the feelings we share.

From the roots to the stars, let joy begin,

Welfare of you, in love's ability to win.

Oh baby, I won't judge you,

In my arms, your worries will find a view.

I'll conserve your trust, filter your dreams,

Clean up the threats, and stitch up the seams.

You've got the strength, to find your way,

From me to you, I'll never sway.

As your best friend, forever I'll be,

A star guiding you, endlessly.

Oh baby, I won't judge you,

In my arms, your worries will find a view.

I'll conserve your trust, filter your dreams,

Clean up the threats, and stitch up the seams.

So baby, I decided to be a star so bright,

Like the pole star, steadfast in the night.

Till eternity, my promise stands true,

Oh baby, I won't judge you.

Yes, baby, I won't judge you.

# About the Author

Radhika Kailash Moryani is an artist of words, weaving poetry, reflections, and stories drawn from the quiet corners of her heart. A graphic designer by profession and a dreamer by nature, she began writing in 2017 as a way to give voice to emotions too deep to remain unspoken. What started as scattered thoughts slowly became a journey of self-discovery and love.

Her book, I Am There, is not just a collection of words but a mirror of her inner world—of struggles, resilience, and the gentle blooming of hope. Deeply connected to birds, animals, and the natural world, Radhika writes with simplicity and sincerity, believing that love, in its truest form, begins with oneself.

An introvert with an empathetic soul, she dedicates her work to reminding readers that even in the mire of life's challenges, one can bloom beautifully.

Through I Am There, she opens her heart to the world, offering her journey as a quiet companion to anyone seeking courage, healing, and self-love.

**ALWAYS BLESSED, GRATEFUL & THANKFUL**

www.ingramcontent.com/pod-product-compliance
Lightning Source LLC
Chambersburg PA
CBHW062147160726
48282CB00027B/952